PEACEFUL
PROTESTERS

Aung San Suu Kyi

Peaceful Resistance to the Burmese Military Junta

Patrice Sherman

Cavendish
Square

New York

Published in 2018 by Cavendish Square Publishing, LLC
243 5th Avenue, Suite 136, New York, NY 10016

Library of Congress Cataloging-in-Publication Data

Names: Sherman, Patrice, author.
Title: Aung San Suu Kyi : peaceful resistance to the Burmese military junta / Patrice Sherman.
Description: New York : Cavendish Square Publishing, [2018] | Series: Peaceful protesters | Includes bibliographical references and index.
Identifiers: LCCN 2017019292 (print) | LCCN 2017020170 (ebook) | ISBN 9781502631107 (library bound) | ISBN 9781502633989 (Paperback) | ISBN 9781502631114 (E-book)
Subjects: LCSH: Aung San Suu Kyi--Juvenile literature. | Women political activists--Burma--Biography--Juvenile literature. | Women political prisoners--Burma--Biography--Juvenile literature. | Women Nobel Prize winners--Burma--Biography--Juvenile literature. | Democracy--Burma--Juvenile literature. | Burma--Politics and government--1988---Juvenile literature.
Classification: LCC DS530.53.A85 (ebook) | LCC DS530.53.A85 S54 2018 (print) | DDC 959.105/4092 [B] --dc23
LC record available at https://lccn.loc.gov/2017019292

Editorial Director: David McNamara
Editor: Caitlyn Miller
Copy Editor: Nathan Heidelberger
Associate Art Director: Amy Greenan
Designer: Alan Sliwinski
Production Coordinator: Karol Szymczuk
Photo Research: J8 Media

CONTENTS

ONE   The Lady 5

TWO   Myanmar: Hope and Struggle 23

THREE   The Path to Leadership 49

FOUR   The Long Fight for Freedom 73

Chronology 99

Glossary 101

Further Information 103

Bibliography 105

Index 109

About the Author 112

Burmese politician and human rights activist Aung San Suu Kyi shortly after she was released from house arrest in 1995

CHAPTER ONE

The Lady

April is a hot, dry month in Myanmar. It is a time when people wait anxiously for the wet **monsoon** that brings heavy rain in May, a time when food is scarce, sleep is difficult, and tempers are likely to flare. On April 5, 1989, a convoy of cars rumbled down a dusty road along the Irrawaddy River towards the town of Danubyu in Myanmar's southern delta region. Danubyu is a place of some importance. It serves as the region's capital and maintains a busy harbor where boats fan out to the many smaller towns and villages situated on the river's banks. The delta region had once been rich in rice, and seizing Danubyu from Myanmar's king had been crucial to Britain's conquest of Myanmar, which began in the 1820s. That April day, however, Danubyu was to become famous for a very different style of confrontation.

A New Election

The travelers, numbering about fifty in all, represented Myanmar's newly founded National League for Democracy (NLD). For several months they had been holding rallies throughout the countryside to promote the league's candidates in the upcoming election. Everywhere they went they were met by enthusiastic supporters, most of them poor farmers or small tradespeople. Myanmar's ordinary citizens had suffered cruelly under the rule of the military **junta.** The nation once known as the "rice basket" of Southeast Asia was now one of the poorest in the world.

The summer of 1988 had proved a turning point. Anti-government protests led by students flared up in Myanmar's capital city, Yangon. These demonstrations were swiftly and violently put down by the army, or Tatmadaw, as it was officially known in Myanmar. The **dissidents** refused to disband. A cycle of uprisings followed by brutal suppression ensued, and for a while it seemed the country was in a complete tailspin, headed toward chaos. Then, on July 23, General Ne Win, Myanmar's dictator, amazed the nation by announcing that he was stepping

A Note About Geographic Names and Locations

Dating back to the British conquest of the nation, Aung San Suu Kyi's country was known as Burma. Additionally, the former capital city, Yangon, was known as Rangoon. Many people use the names Burma and Rangoon today. In fact, Suu Kyi still calls her country Burma. However, the names were officially changed by the State Law and Order Restoration Council (SLORC) in 1989, so you'll find the names Myanmar and Yangon used throughout this book.

People from Myanmar are still generally referred to as "Burmese," despite the name change. Also of note, though Yangon was the country's capital during the events discussed in the book, the country built a new capital city, called Nay Pyi Taw (or Naypyidaw), and relocated the capital there in 2006.

down. He would hand the government over to another general, and elections would be held for a new parliament. Ne Win did not exactly promise democracy, nor did he state when and how the elections would take place. The protests and violent repression continued, but now people at least had hope. There was an opening, however slim, for change.

Within a few weeks of Ne Win's announcement, dozens of political parties sprang up. Myanmar had a large parliament of 492 seats. Under Ne Win, all had been occupied by one party, the Burma Socialist Programme Party (BSPP), founded when the general had seized power in 1962. Encouraged by the promise of open elections, groups large and small began to organize campaigns. But none attracted as much attention as the NLD. Wherever its representatives traveled, people greeted them with flowers, songs, and waving flags. It was not just the party's ideas that drew them; they came for one individual: **Daw** Suu. *Daw* means "aunt" in Burmese, and it is a title of both honor and affection. Daw Suu's full name is Aung San Suu Kyi, and if anyone could bring true democracy to Myanmar, people believed, it was their beloved Daw.

A Campaign of Peace and Strength

The army had not failed to note the growing popularity of Aung San Suu Kyi and her party. Over the previous year, many of her supporters had been arrested and charged with crimes they did not commit. When she traveled, she and her companions were often harassed by soldiers. Sometimes the road would be barricaded by troops, and the NLD cars would be stranded for hours in some remote location. Other times, the appearance of armed troops might bring a public meeting to an abrupt halt. The threat of violence always hung in the air.

Nevertheless, Suu Kyi was not armed, nor did she allow her supporters to carry weapons. She refused to meet violence with violence. Her "bodyguards" were unarmed students who had sworn to protect her even if all they could do was place themselves between her and whatever weapons might be pointed her way. So far, it had not come to that. In fact, the party seemed on a roll to victory that could not be stopped.

Supporters turned out by the thousands wherever she went. The international press had taken notice, too. "Once the waters of a revolution start flowing, you can't push them back forever," Suu Kyi had told a reporter from the *New York Times* who had come to interview her in January 1989. The NLD rapidly became one of the largest political parties in the country, boasting between three million and five million members. Its support was especially strong in the delta region south and east of Yangon, exactly where Suu Kyi found herself on April 5.

Yet on that day, few supporters turned out to greet her. Rather than cheering crowds with flowers, only a few frightened faces peered from doorways and windows. Suu Kyi and her fellow travelers were brought to a halt by a young army officer who told them that due to recent unrest, the town of Danubyu was under **martial law**. No open-air assemblies could be held; anyone holding such a meeting would be shot. They would have to turn back. Undeterred, Suu Kyi asked if she could address a meeting indoors at the local NLD headquarters. She promised there would be no unrest or lawless behavior. Perhaps the officer was a bit ashamed or confused by her calm and courteous attitude, for to everyone's surprise, he agreed. Over eighty people crammed into the small room occupied by the headquarters. Many more had to be sent away, but everyone remained peaceful.

Refusing to Back Down

After Suu Kyi finished her speech, the visitors proceeded on foot to the docks, where they planned to take boats to visit the nearby villages along the riverbank. This time the officer was not deferential. Suu Kyi and her followers' route was lined with armed soldiers, and the officer followed them in a vehicle, warning them that it was a violation of martial law to walk in a large group. If they did not disperse, they would be shot. One of Suu Kyi's colleagues later recalled that although soldiers had often ordered them about, this was the first time they had been threatened so directly with death. Still, Suu Kyi remained calm. She looked upon the soldiers as if they were her sons, nephews, or brothers. She even stopped to speak to one who seemed hesitant to obey commands. "Hey," she reminded him gently, "they are telling you to load, aren't you going to, soldier?" Her lack of fear only enraged the officer further. He had issued his gravest threat only to be humiliated in front of his men by a "mere" woman.

As the NLD group boarded their boats, Suu Kyi promised the officer they world return well before the town curfew at dark. She had told her supporters that she would spend the night in town, and she didn't want to disappoint them.

Suu Kyi and her companions spent the rest of the afternoon visiting several villages where they ate, listened to music and poetry, and talked to the residents about their concerns and the upcoming election. True to her word, Suu Kyi had the group back at Danubyu by six o'clock in the evening, when the sky was still light. Not surprisingly, the soldiers were waiting for them on the dock. Several members of the group wanted to continue down the river and disembark in a safe location, but Suu Kyi remained firm. Retreat would signal weakness. She was not violent, but neither was she weak. Army professionals, she knew, often thought that those who rejected violence were weak. The only way she could demonstrate the difference was by acting on her beliefs.

As the NLD group walked back through the town, the soldiers began to push and shove. They wanted their victims to fight back and give them an excuse to fire their weapons. Suu Kyi signaled her followers to remain orderly. When the soldiers told them they could not walk in the street, she asked her followers to walk by the side of the road. When told they could not walk in twos and threes, she asked that they walk single file. The soldiers backed off but did not lower their weapons. At one point Suu Kyi approached a soldier, telling him with a smile, "You really shouldn't bully me so much. You must let us pass." He lowered his gun.

The town appeared deserted, but here and there cries of "Long live Daw Aung San" and "Let them pass" rang out from darkened windows. Accounts about what happened next vary. Win Thein, a student who acted as Suu Kyi's chauffeur and main bodyguard, later recalled that near the marketplace the group approached yet another group of soldiers kneeling in formation, their rifles aimed straight ahead. Win Thein had been walking in front of Suu Kyi carrying the NLD flag. At the sight of the soldiers, Suu Kyi gestured to her other followers to remain behind her. Then she stepped out into the middle of the road, in clear view of the marksmen. Win Thein stayed in front of her; she asked him to keep on walking.

The officer who had threatened them before now made ready to make good on his threats. He commenced the order to fire. Win Thein knew this was no empty gesture. He had participated in demonstrations in Yangon and had seen his comrades murdered by government troops. But he had sworn to protect Suu Kyi. He kept on walking in front of her, step by step, his eyes closed, waiting for the sound of gunfire, certain he would die at any moment.

"Don't do it!" he heard someone yell. "Don't do it Myint U!" Win Thein opened his eyes and saw a senior officer running up to the younger officer, ordering him to stand down. Win Thein looked behind him. Suu Kyi was no longer there. She had simply kept walking, passing him by. She had made herself the main target, approaching the soldiers until she was only inches from their gun barrels. Now he saw her slipping between them as if they were nothing more than grass or trees.

"I noticed that some of them, one or two, were actually shaking and muttering to themselves," Suu Kyi later recalled. "But I don't know whether it was out of hatred or nervousness." She dismissed any notion that she had been particularly brave. "You can't make up your mind in advance what you'll do," she told an interviewer. "When it comes to the crunch, when you're actually faced with that kind of danger, you have to make up your mind on the spot." Her only concern, she insisted, was for her friends. If the soldiers really wanted to kill her, it would be easier, she thought, if they had one target rather than many.

Stepping into History

To those who had known her growing up, Suu Kyi did not seem like someone who would one day be facing down armed soldiers in a remote region of Myanmar. Though born in Myanmar, she had lived abroad since the

Suu Kyi graduated from Oxford University's St. Hugh's College for Women in 1967.

age of fifteen, first in India and then in Great Britain and the United States. She had attended Britain's prestigious St. Hugh's College for Women, part of Oxford University, and worked as a secretary for the United Nations in New York City. She liked literature, especially the novels of Jane Austen, and enjoyed playing the piano. She even knew a bit about ikebana, the Japanese art of flower arranging. Friends described her as kind and friendly, if a bit proper or "straight-laced." She was interested in other people, rarely acted impulsively, and gave the impression that she thought things over a great deal before she spoke.

A Love Story

By her early forties, she had settled in back in Oxford, England, the wife of a college professor and a stay-at-home mom to her two young sons. A close friend remembers seeing her bicycling through the town with grocery bags of fruit and vegetables hanging from the handlebars. Once home, she would prepare delicious Burmese meals for family and friends. Suu Kyi's husband, Michael Aris, was a scholar of Tibetan Buddhism. When people came to visit, conversation often revolved around Eastern history and religion. As her children grew older, Suu Kyi began to think about going back to school herself to study Burmese literature. She also wanted to spend more time writing. All in all, she seemed destined for a quiet life.

Still, the fate of her homeland was never far from her mind. When she was twenty-six, she had written a letter to her future husband. It was a love letter of sorts—not about her love for him, though she did love him deeply, but about her love for her country. "I only ask one thing," she wrote. "That should my people need me, you would help me do my duty by them." That duty, she continued, might involve long and painful separation:

"

Sometimes I am beset by fears that circumstances and national considerations might tear us apart just when we are so happy in each other ... And yet such fears are so futile and inconsequential: if we love and cherish each other as much as we can while we can, I am sure love and compassion will triumph in the end.

Essentially, Suu Kyi was telling her fiancé that should she ever be asked to choose between him and her country, her country came first. Another man might have walked away, angry and insulted. But Michael Aris was the perfect match for Suu Kyi. He knew that despite her quiet exterior, she was a fierce and passionate person. He loved her all the more for her devotion to her people and was ready to accept the consequences, whatever they happened to be.

Duty and Commitment

Suu Kyi was not superstitious. She did not believe in what other people called fate or destiny, but she did believe in duty. Everyone had a duty in life. It might not make for a good life, but no one could turn away: her father had done his duty even though it had cost him his life.

General Aung San had died when Suu Kyi was barely two years old. She did not remember her father, but she had heard stories about him. She knew that he had founded Myanmar's army and negotiated the country's independence from Britain after World War II. People called him the "father of modern Myanmar." Decades after his death, he was still regarded as the nation's greatest hero. Growing up, Suu Kyi always hoped she would be as brave as he.

The call to serve her country, however, did not come until she was middle-aged. Even then, the opportunity presented itself in an unexpected manner. In March of 1988, Suu Kyi received a call telling her that her mother was very ill. Suu Kyi immediately flew to Myanmar to care for her mother, assuming she would return to England once her mother's condition stabilized. Instead, she found herself engulfed in a raging storm of protest. The streets of Yangon seemed to seethe with anti-government sentiment. Suu Kyi was well aware of the protests and the government's brutal response, but she felt that she was too busy caring for her mother to become involved.

Once the protesters learned that General Aung San's daughter was in the city, they begged her to speak at one of their rallies. Suu Kyi hesitated. She was still not sure that this was the moment to step into the spotlight as her father's heir. The doctors had told her that her mother was dying. She had two children who needed her. Hesitantly, she agreed to speak at an outdoor meeting in September.

Her speech was not particularly dramatic. She was not a firebrand shouting slogans. She did not issue any call to arms. Instead, she spoke in measured tones about democracy and the need for all of Myanmar's people to come together and form a new kind of government. Her words appealed to those who had remained on the edge of the protests, unsure if they wanted to become involved in violence. She seemed to have a knack for connecting with people in a very natural way. Suu Kyi didn't sound like a politician, but like an ordinary woman who cared about her country. People who had come out of curiosity to see the General Aung San's daughter began to listen and appreciate Suu Kyi for her own sake.

By the end of the year, there was no question of her returning to Britain. The prodemocracy movement needed her too much. Her life was now characterized by feverish activity; when she was not traveling, she was holding meetings in her home. Someone suggested that she make a tour of the delta region before the oncoming rainy season made the roads impassable. In early April 1989, a little over a year after leaving England, Suu Kyi was on her way to the town of Danubyu on the banks of the Irrawaddy River.

A Warrior's Daughter

Some moments in history become iconic—that is, they come to symbolize something larger than themselves. As far as Suu Kyi was concerned, her confrontation with the would-be firing squad in Danubyu was just another episode in the campaign for democracy in Myanmar. Yet within a matter of days, she had become a legend. She was invested with almost supernatural powers: she was the woman who could stare down bullets, who could face loaded rifles and overcome them, armed with nothing more than the power of her beliefs. There were no cameras that day in Danubyu, but millions of people heard about the encounter and saw her in their imaginations—a slight, almost frail woman wearing the traditional Burmese blouse and skirt, or *aingyi* and *longyi*, a white flower in her hair, walking unafraid toward rifles aimed at her very heart.

Just as Suu Kyi had become larger than life that day, the soldiers, too, acquired symbolic importance. They seemed to represent all the forces arrayed against the

USE YOUR LIBERTY TO PROMOTE OURS

FREE

In June 2009, Burmese prodemocracy activists held demonstrations calling for the release of Suu Kyi from house arrest and the release of her supporters from prison.

people of Myanmar, and even more, against all those who suffered under tyranny worldwide. Her actions conveyed that **nonviolence** was powerful, that it could win even the toughest battles.

Over the next twenty-five years, Aung San Suu Kyi would become one of the most famous women on earth. Her image would be splashed across newspapers throughout the world. Even those who knew little about

Myanmar would come to know about the courageous woman with the flower in her hair. They would call her "The Steel Orchid," "The Iron Butterfly," or simply "The Lady." She would receive some of the world's highest honors, including the Nobel Peace Prize and the US Congressional Medal of Honor.

Strangely enough, at the very time her fame soared, she would also be one of the world's least known citizens, locked away as a political prisoner for years at a time behind the gates of her own house. She would be cut off from the press that praised her, conspicuously absent from the ceremonies that honored her, isolated from family and friends, her voice almost entirely silenced. Yet the more the government of Myanmar tried to render her invisible, the greater her fame grew. Laura Bush, First Lady and wife of President George W. Bush, launched a campaign on her behalf. Supporters in Ireland celebrated her birthday with rallies calling for her release. A poster several stories high demanding that she be set free adorned a government building in Rome.

A Complicated Legacy

It is not easy to be a living legend, and once freedom finally came, Suu Kyi had to shoulder a very different set of problems, often facing criticism and condemnation from the same people who had praised her earlier. Some would accuse her of being a fraud. They would come to believe she had deliberately misled the public about her devotion to **human rights** and nonviolence. Others would simply acknowledge that Suu Kyi was not a saint but an ordinary human being, flawed like any other. If the story of Suu Kyi teaches us anything, it is how complicated the fight for human rights can be. It is easy to idealize those who practice nonviolence, but nonviolence cannot be carried out by heroes alone. If it were, it would be of little use. Flawless heroes are few and far between. In order to be effective, nonviolence must be adopted by people—ordinary, complicated, flawed, and difficult people, people like Aung San Suu Kyi.

Beginning with her release in 2010, Suu Kyi moved from protesting those in power to possessing considerable political power herself. Once an outsider, she became part of the political establishment, serving as her country's state counsel and foreign minister. In her new position of power, she has made some controversial decisions. But, as she told the press in 2013, "I have never done anything just for popularity." She has always insisted that she did not set out to be a hero and certainly not a saint. "I have a temper," she acknowledges, and sometimes it gets the better of her. If those around her had underestimated her combative spirit, she never did. She believed she came by her fierceness quite naturally. It was part of her heritage, something she had to live up to almost from the moment she was born, for she was, above all, a warrior's daughter.

Shwedagon Pagoda is one of the most sacred Buddhist sites in Myanmar. Also known as the Great Dragon Pagoda, it is located in the city of Yangon.

CHAPTER TWO

Myanmar:
Hope and Struggle

Myanmar is the largest nation in Southeast Asia. Shaped roughly like a kite, its top half appears to be squeezed between Myanmar's two largest neighbors, China and India, both of which have exerted a strong influence on its history and culture. The "tail" of the kite reaches down into the peninsula occupied by Malaysia and borders the Andaman Sea.

Myanmar has a rich and diverse culture. The population consists of eight main ethnic groups. The largest of these is the Burmans, also called the Bamar, who make up about 68 percent of the population and from whom the country got its former name, Burma. The second-largest

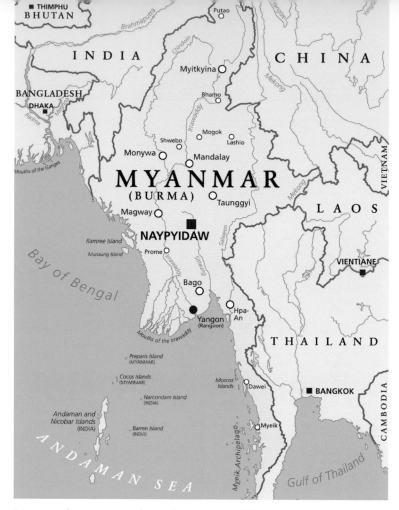

Myanmar became an independent state in 1948.

group is the Shan, about 9 percent of the population, followed by the Karen (or Kayin) with about 8 percent. The remaining 15 percent of the population is divided among the Rakhine, Chin (or Chinese), Kayah, Kachin, and Mon. Within these main groups are many smaller ethnic groups.

Burmese, spoken by the Burmans, is the main language, but there are around thirty-five other languages in the country. Approximately 90 percent of Myanmar's people are Buddhist. Slightly more than 6 percent are Christian, and about 4.3 percent are Muslim. A small number of people still practice local pagan religions.

Myanmar's diversity has been both a strength and a weakness. Unity under a single government has proved difficult. Ethnic tensions have always run high, and disputes over land, natural resources, rivers, and roads have frequently erupted into bloody tribal warfare.

The Burman kings were the first to conquer the region, establishing a **dynasty** in the late thirteenth century. Under their rule, Buddhism became the main religion, and the country became known as the Land of the Golden **Pagodas**. Over the next three centuries, the kingdom would expand to include areas to the north and west. European explorers first arrived by boat in the 1500s. Impressed by Myanmar's rich resources, they set up trade in teakwood, teas, spices, and precious gemstones.

Myanmar Under Colonial Rule

Britain emerged as the leading **colonial power** in the nineteenth century and sought to take control over both Myanmar and India through a series of wars and invasions. British colonial rule in India began in 1857, and they completed their conquest of Myanmar, begun in the 1820s, in 1885. Under British rule, Myanmar became a province

Britain completed its conquest of Myanmar in 1885. Many people from India worked in Myanmar as civil servants under British rule.

of India. Because they had already trained Indians to work as civil servants, the British imported people from India, most of them Hindus, to serve as bureaucrats and administrators for Myanmar's colonial government. This practice rankled the Buddhist Burmese and led to increasing religious tensions. In addition, the Burmese felt that Britain favored Chinese merchants in the western part of the state over the native people. Britain regarded Myanmar as a trade link between India and China, but few Burmese profited from the trade. By the end of the nineteenth century, Myanmar was the world's leading exporter of rice, yet people in remote provinces often went hungry. Rebellions broke out frequently, only to be swiftly and brutally put down.

While British rule was oppressive, the British also brought new ideas. English became a second language in Myanmar. The British established a university at Yangon where young men of the upper classes could train as civil servants and lawyers. Through their studies, these students became acquainted with the concepts of democracy, parliamentary procedure, and representative government. Above all, the British brought with them the European notion of the nation state.

By the early twentieth century, a wave of **nationalism** had begun to spread throughout Asia. In China, Sun Yat-sen overthrew the European-backed Qing dynasty and founded the first Republic of China in 1912. Mahatma Gandhi launched his first campaign of nonviolent protests against the British occupation of India in 1919. The Vietnamese communist leader

Rangoon College, shown here in the early 1900s, was founded by the British. It would eventually become the University of Yangon.

Ho Chi Minh organized the Vietnam Revolutionary Youth League in the 1920s to free his country from French rule. National movements often grow up around a single leader. One strong individual can give people focus and hope. Myanmar found its leader in a young man from the district of Magwe called Aung San.

Born Under a Lucky Star

According to his horoscope, Aung San was destined for leadership from birth, for the astrologer his parents consulted assured them that February 13, 1915, was an especially auspicious day for an infant boy to come into the world. Aung San was the youngest of eight children. His father served as a minor official in the district government, and his mother managed the family farm. Although they were not wealthy, Aung San's parents valued education and earned enough money to send their children to school at the local monastery.

If they had hoped to see early signs of greatness in Aung San, however, his mother and father must have been very disappointed. He did not speak until he was nearly four years old and showed so little interest in school his parents gave up and let him stay home. At the age of eight, he could barely read or write. He could be stubborn and wild one moment, yet charming and entertaining the next. As the baby of the family, he was spoiled and knew how to get his own way: when his mother refused to buy him sweets, he convinced his older siblings to buy them for him.

The Education of Aung San

Primary schools in Myanmar were at the time maintained by Buddhist monks who taught their pupils religion, Burmese literature, history, and mathematics. When a male student finished his course of studies, he underwent a Buddhist initiation rite, living at the monastery for a few months to practice meditation and learn humility, obedience, self-restraint, and other traditional Buddhist values. When Aung San was about ten, his favorite older brother left for the monastery. As part of the initiation ceremony, he rode a white horse. Aung San immediately told his parents he wanted to ride a white horse, too. His mother pointed out that only initiates to the monastery could ride the white horse, and only those who finished school could become initiates. If he wanted to ride a white horse, he would have to go to school first. Aung San thought it over. He would go to school.

Once he enrolled in school, Aung San amazed his teachers with his passion for learning. Suddenly books fascinated him. He skipped several grades, and at the age of thirteen, he led his class in academics. By then, he was less interested in riding a white horse than he was in learning English. He longed to read the works of the great English poets and novelists, but English was not taught at his school. If he wanted to learn English, he would have to leave home. In 1930, he won a scholarship to the National School in the city of Yenangyaung. National schools functioned as high schools in Myanmar and taught students in both English and Burmese.

At that time, Myanmar was experiencing a wave of nationalism, and Yenangyaung was a center of political activity. Aung San joined the debating club and worked as editor of the school magazine. In one of his debates, he cited Abraham Lincoln as one of his favorite heroes. Though he loved literature, politics now began to absorb him entirely. "Politics means your everyday life," he later told his followers. "It is how you eat, sleep, work, and live ... You may not think about politics, but politics thinks about you."

After graduating from the National School in 1932, Aung San enrolled in the University of Yangon (then called the University of Rangoon). There he quickly became involved in political clubs where people discussed Marxism, **socialism**, communism, and other political ideas. Aung San didn't promote any of these "isms" himself. His main interest was Burmese independence, and he was willing to explore any philosophy that might help his country achieve that goal.

His devotion to his cause made him something of a campus "wild man." While the others kept their hair short and wore neat, professional-looking clothes, Aung

San let his hair grow long and wore the same clothes day in and day out until they were ragged and torn. He did not have time, he said, for barbers and tailors, and he preferred to spend his money on books. To improve his English, he would spend hours alone outdoors, reciting famous speeches to an audience of trees and bushes. Fellow students described him as "crude" and "raw." These same qualities gave him courage. When asked why he did not sleep under a mosquito net, he replied that he assumed his politics would eventually land him in prison, and he needed to get used to doing without luxuries.

In 1936, he led a student strike against corrupt university officials that almost got him expelled. The confrontation with authority only exhilarated him. After finishing his bachelor's degree, Aung San enrolled in the university's law school, mostly to convince his parents to let him stay in the city. His real goal was politics. He joined an organization called the Dobama Asiayone, which translates loosely as "We Burmese Association," and he became its secretary-general.

Aung San Rises to the National Stage

During the late 1930s, Myanmar entered a downward economic spiral. People could no longer afford rice, and wages declined. In 1939, Aung San helped lead a strike of farm laborers, oil workers, miners, students, and monks. The British police opened fire on the strikers, killing seventeen people. Aung San was arrested and taken to prison. Public protests forced the British to release him after two weeks—he was now a national figure. He would not give up until Myanmar had become independent of all foreign rule. "To be a subject nation," he declared, "is like someone lost in a forest after midnight in the waning moon." All he wanted was to lead his people out of that forest to freedom.

The General

Aung San is known as the father of modern Myanmar. He negotiated its independence from Britain in 1947.

Aung San must have known about Gandhi's philosophy of nonviolence in India, but he did not seem to be drawn to it. Instead, he turned to Japan. Japan was one of the few nations in Asia that had never been colonized by Western powers. Aung San was impressed by the fact that the Japanese had always dealt with Westerners as equals. The Japanese called their nation the Land of the Rising Sun, and it was certainly the rising power in Asia. The government believed in **fascism**, an extreme form of nationalism that consisted of a powerful military force led by a single dictator. Japan had an emperor, but most of the power was concentrated in the hands of its prime minister, General Tojo.

It may seem odd that someone who was as devoted to democracy as Aung San would admire a military dictatorship, but Aung San saw Japan's policy as "Asia for the Asians." In the late 1930s, the Japanese government had made it clear that Japan wanted to force foreign powers out of Asia. Aung San believed that if he helped Japan push Britain out of Myanmar, the Japanese would help Myanmar become an independent state.

In 1940, Aung San traveled to Japan and met with officials who promised arms and military training in return for Burmese support against the British. A year later, Aung San and thirty of his colleagues, armed with Japanese weapons, formed the Burma Independence Army. Aung San became the general, or *bogyoke*. For the rest of his life, he would be known as Bogyoke Aung San, or simply "The Bogyoke."

In 1942, Japan seized Myanmar from the British. For his aid in the campaign, Aung San received a medal from Japan's emperor and was promoted to war minister of Myanmar under the new Japanese regime. The British considered him a traitor and put a price on his head.

It did not take long for Aung San to become disappointed with his Japanese allies, who regarded Myanmar's people as inferior races. They forced peasants to labor on construction projects, confiscated rice and other natural resources, and in general treated the native population with brutality and contempt. Japan, Aung San realized, wanted only to expand its own empire. The Japanese had no intention of allowing Myanmar or any of their conquered territories to become independent states.

Aung San decided the only possible course of action was to shift his loyalty to the British. In November of 1943, he traveled in secret to a British army encampment in the mountains of northern Myanmar to offer his help in defeating the Japanese. The British commander did not exactly welcome him. The entry of the United States into the war in late 1941 had guaranteed a Japanese defeat. Japan had already lost a series of significant battles to US forces. It was only a matter of time before Japan surrendered Myanmar, too. The British commander pointed all this out to Aung San, adding, "You only came to us because we are winning."

"It wouldn't be much good coming to you if you weren't," Aung San replied. To his surprise, the commander laughed. He appreciated Aung San's honesty, and the two men made a deal. From then on, Aung San and his army would be working for the British. Turning against the Japanese was risky, though. Aung San and his men acted as if they were still allied to the Japanese, accompanying Japanese forces into the jungle to fight British troops and then turning on them once they were concealed behind the trees. Had the Japanese discovered that he was aiding the enemy, Aung San would have been executed. Yet it wasn't his own safety he feared for; by 1944, he had a family to protect.

The Start of a Family Dynasty

Aung San had never shown much interest in dating when he was in college. Politics came first in his life, and he had little time for romance. Marriage, he feared, would only distract him from his commitment to his country. The summer of 1942 changed his mind about that. Illness had landed him in a hospital in Yangon, and Aung San was a difficult patient because he hated weakness of any kind. He wanted to be back out fighting, not lying in bed. The doctor asked the hospital's strictest nurse to take charge of him. Her name was Khin Kyi. At thirty, she was three years older than the Bogyoke, a confident, proud, and courageous woman who had already faced her share of danger. Early in the war, Khin Kyi had helped smuggle Indian nationals out of Myanmar to Kolkata, India (then known as Calcutta). The Japanese considered Indians to be British subjects and declared that aiding them was treason. Khin Kyi didn't care. As a nurse, she was committed to helping all those in need, no matter what country they belonged to.

If the Japanese did not frighten her, she surely wasn't going to allow herself to be bullied by Aung San. He was rude, demanding, and impatient. She was firm, dignified, and kind. After a few arguments, he gave her his grudging respect, and then the respect turned to love. Once he was discharged from the hospital, Aung San asked Khin Kyi to marry him, but Khin Kyi hesitated. She, too, had avoided romantic entanglements when she was young and dedicated herself to her career. Yet Aung San loved her because of her independent streak, not despite it. They married on September 6, 1942.

Khin Kyi bore a son, Aung San Oo, in 1943. A year later, she had a second son, Aung San Lin. In the spring of 1945, the Japanese made their last stand in Yangon. Fighting broke out in the streets between Japanese and Burmese forces. Allied planes bombarded the city every night. Khin Kyi, pregnant with her third child, was forced to flee to the countryside with her two little sons. Three members of the Burmese army, disguised as peasants, went with her. They almost didn't make it; as they approached a small fishing village, a Japanese soldier stopped the party and demanded to know where they were going. Khin Kyi coolly replied that they only wanted to buy fish. Amused, the soldier let them pass. He was going to the same village to buy fish also.

Khin Kyi returned to Yangon when the Japanese withdrew from Myanmar in May 1945. There, Khin Kyi and her children reunited with Aung San and a new life began. On June 19, 1945, Khin Kyi gave birth; she named the infant girl Aung San Suu Kyi, which means "Strange Collection of Bright Victories."

Aung San's Dream of Democracy

The aftermath of the war was a busy and happy time for Aung San and Khin Kyi. Aung San immediately began to work for his long-held dream of independence for Myanmar. Myanmar was still a British colony, but Britain now granted the Burmese a measure of control over national affairs. In 1946, Aung San was appointed deputy chairman of the Executive Council of Myanmar. He also became the president of the Anti-Fascist People's Freedom League (AFPFL), a prodemocracy political party that he and his followers had organized in 1945. In January

Aung San and his wife, Khin Kyi, with their children in 1946. Aung San Suu Kyi (*far right*) was born on June 19, 1945.

of 1947, Aung San traveled to Britain and negotiated a treaty that would grant Myanmar complete independence within a year. That April, AFPFL won 196 out of the 202 seats in the election for Myanmar's first parliament. The assembly was charged with drawing up a constitution for the new nation and choosing a prime minister. As leader of AFPFL, Aung San was in line to become head of Myanmar's first democratic government.

Meanwhile, Khin Kyi devoted herself to raising their children and helping her husband with his political campaign. Despite his busy schedule, Aung San was a loving and playful father. He liked buying gifts for his children and returned from Britain with a large doll for Suu Kyi that she still had many years later, when she returned to Myanmar as an adult woman.

Though AFPFL had become the leading party, Myanmar's many political, ethnic, and regional factions threatened to undermine the new government. Aung San used his position to promote unity. He had emerged from the war a popular hero, but he was not without rivals. On July 19, 1947, while he was presiding over a cabinet meeting in Yangon, a group of eight men broke into the room and opened fire. Aung San and six others were killed. He was thirty-two years old. Upon receiving the news, Khin Kyi insisted on preparing her husband's body for burial herself. In the same hospital where they had met, she washed his corpse and cleaned his wounds.

The ringleader of the assassination was a man named U Saw. He and five others were convicted of murder and executed a year later—the reason for their actions never became completely clear. U Saw regarded Aung San as an upstart who had seized power unfairly, and he possibly blamed Aung San for an attempt on his own life that had been made a few weeks before the assassination.

On January 4, 1948, Myanmar officially became an independent state. The parliament named U Nu, a supporter of Aung San, prime minister. One of his first acts was to designate July 19 as Martyrs' Day in memory of Aung San. In April, Khin Kyi had her husband's remains reinterred at the Shwedagon Pagoda, the most sacred of Myanmar's Buddhist temples. Thousands of mourners attended the ceremony to honor their Bogyoke. Forty years later, thousands would gather again to hear the Bogyoke's daughter speak from the steps of the same temple, calling for the freedom her father had so loved.

Aung San Suu Kyi, Unafraid of the Dark

As an adult, Suu Kyi would sometimes tell people that when she was a small child she would force herself to get out of bed late at night while the rest of the family slept. Silently, she would tiptoe downstairs and look into the dining room and the kitchen. Only when she had assured herself that no monsters lurked there would she

Aung San Suu Kyi around the age of six

creep back upstairs. She did not remember her father, for he had died when she was barely two years old. But her mother spoke of him frequently. Aung San had been a brave man, Khin Kyi told her children. He had hated cowardice more than anything. Suu Kyi wanted to be brave, too; she did not want to be afraid of the dark.

The loss of her father was not the only tragedy to mark her childhood. Suu Kyi was especially close to her second-oldest brother, Aung San Lin. One day, when she was about five, he went out to retrieve a toy that had fallen into the pond behind their house. His feet became entangled in some muddy roots, and he drowned. Suu Kyi rarely talked about her brother's death, but those who knew her as a child often remarked upon how serious she seemed to be. She was not fearful, but she already knew that the world could be a sad and dangerous place. After her brother's death, the family moved to a house on 54 University Avenue in Yangon. It would be Suu Kyi's home when she returned to Myanmar in 1988, a house that would become both her shelter and her prison.

Khin Kyi's commitment to her country was as strong as her husband's had been. After Aung San's assassination, she had gone back to work not just because she needed to earn money but also to show people that she was not afraid. She wanted to do her part to keep the Bogyoke's dream of democracy alive. In 1948, she became director of the National Women's and Children's Welfare Board. Prime Minister U Nu appointed her head of the government's Social Planning Commission in 1952. In addition, she organized women voters and made her home a center for political discussions and meetings. Many years later, when a reporter asked Suu Kyi how she had acquired her strength and resilience, she joked that she had "chosen" the right parents. Most people thought she was talking about her famous father, but she knew her mother was an individual of rare courage, too. At a time when few women pursued careers, Khin Kyi set an example for her daughter.

It was not always an easy example to live up to. Khin Kyi had high standards. She expected Suu Kyi to be polite, well groomed, and studious. If guests dropped by, Suu Kyi could not come down to greet them unless she was immaculately attired in clean, freshly ironed clothes, with every strand of her long black hair neatly braided and in place. But if she wasn't exactly warm, Khin Kyi could still treat her daughter with patience and respect. Suu Kyi loved to ask questions. She was curious about everything. Khin Kyi worked long hours, yet no matter how late she came home, she always found time to listen to her daughter. When Khin Kyi lay down to rest in her bedroom, Suu Kyi would walk in circles around the bed. Whenever she got to the foot, she would ask her mother another question. "What was water made of?" she demanded. If Khin Kyi did not know the answer, she would encourage Suu Kyi to keep looking until she found it.

Like her father, Suu Kyi was a passionate reader as a child. She attended a local school that had been founded by missionaries and took classes in both English and Burmese. She read everything she could find, including Western comic books—when she could get her hands on them. Her favorite, though, was Sherlock Holmes. Once she discovered Sir Arthur Conan Doyle's famous detective tales, she became a mystery fan for life. She liked the study of motive and wanted to know why people did what they did. Even during the most stressful times of her life, she would always be able to turn to a good mystery novel for much-needed relief and escape.

A Wider World for the Young Lady

In 1960, Suu Kyi's mother was appointed Myanmar's ambassador to India. India was an important post, and serving as Myanmar's ambassador was a high honor for

Khin Kyi. At fifteen, Suu Kyi moved with her mother to New Delhi, where they occupied a large house on 24 Akbar Road in one of the city's wealthiest neighborhoods. As the daughter of an ambassador, Suu Kyi enjoyed luxuries unknown to her in Yangon. She took riding lessons, piano lessons, and learned Japanese flower arranging. Playing the piano became one of her favorite hobbies. She loved classical music, especially Mozart. Like her beloved mystery novels, the piano, too, would continue to offer her comfort during her darkest years.

Suu Kyi attended a private girls' high school in New Delhi for two years and then enrolled in Lady Shri Ram College for Women, part of the University of Delhi. Though she officially majored in political science, she was also drawn to literature. Having discovered Jane Austen and the works of Shakespeare in high school, she longed to try her own hand at creative writing. She had developed a sly sense of humor and surprised her classmates with a witty spoof of Shakespeare's *Antony and Cleopatra*, which they staged for faculty and friends.

While Suu Kyi liked the friends she made at Shri Ram, she also felt frustrated. The college's courses did not challenge her intellectually. Her older brother had enrolled in a British university a few years earlier, and she begged her mother to let her follow him. At first, Khin Kyi was reluctant—England seemed too far away. She wanted her daughter to have a good education, but she was wary of Western culture. The newspapers were filled with stories of young people in London who called themselves "mods" and listened to music called "rock." Photographs showed girls in short skirts and boys sporting long hair. She wondered how Suu Kyi could be exposed to all that and still remain Burmese. Plus, travel was expensive. What would she do during the summer when she could not return to Myanmar? Without saying so out loud, Khin Kyi also implied that she expected Suu Kyi to marry a Burmese man. Moving to England was not the best way for her to find a suitable husband.

Marriage, however, seemed very far from Suu Kyi's mind. She thought she would explore the world for a while, and then, as her mother expected, return to Yangon. She was the Bogyoke's daughter. She felt Burmese with every fiber of her being, and Suu Kyi could not imagine a life apart from her homeland.

Much to Suu Kyi's relief, two of her mother's closest English friends stepped in to help her. Lord Paul and Lady Patricia Gore-Booth offered to serve as her "family" in Britain. Paul Gore-Booth was Britain's ambassador to India; what's more, he was a big fan of Sherlock Holmes and president of England's Sherlock Holmes Society. Suu Kyi already thought of them as her English uncle and aunt. The Gore-Booths assured Khin Kyi that Suu Kyi could spend her vacations with them and they would make sure she always had a home while she lived in England.

NE WIN: DICTATOR OF MYANMAR

Born in 1911, Ne Win initially followed a path similar to that of Aung San. He became involved in the anti-colonial movement as a student at Yangon University and joined the Dobama Asiayone (We Burmese Association) nationalist party in 1931. Ne Win was among the first thirty members of Myanmar's army and fought alongside Aung San, first with and then against the Japanese. After the war, he remained in the army and helped Britain defeat communist rebels in the northern provinces. In 1949, he was appointed the army's commander in chief. During the 1950s, Ne Win turned against a government he saw as weak and ineffective. He believed only the army could fully control the country and only the military had the right to rule. The **coup** of 1962 established him absolute dictator. Ne Win was notoriously superstitious, often making important decisions according to "lucky numbers" and other magical omens. His policies isolated Myanmar from the international community and destroyed the nation's economy. Growing opposition caused him to give up power in 1988. He retired to private life and died in Myanmar in 2002.

Suu Kyi left India for Britain in 1965. She would remain abroad for over twenty years.

The Death of Democracy

Perhaps Khin Kyi finally let her daughter go because she faced a crisis of her own: Myanmar was no longer a democracy. In 1962, General Ne Win had seized power in a military coup. He immediately imprisoned Prime Minister U Nu, dismissed Myanmar's parliament, and suspended the constitution, declaring that "parliamentary democracy was not suitable" for the country. Instead, he instituted a military junta he called the Burma Socialist Programme Party, with himself as chairman. Although Ne Win identified as a socialist, his government really aimed for total state control of all resources and services. A few protests broke out, but they were quickly suppressed. Under Ne Win, the government took control of the media and schools. Free speech ceased to exist. Elections were canceled.

Though Khin Kyi must have been saddened by these developments, she probably wasn't surprised. Myanmar's democracy had always been fragile; Prime Minister U Nu had never fully united the country after the assassination of Aung San. The government exerted little control over the outer provinces, and ethnic and regional conflicts grew. Without a stable government, the economy remained vulnerable and weak. Ne Win did not replace Khin Kyi as ambassador to India. He needed educated and experienced foreign service professionals to help Myanmar interact with the outer world. Khin Kyi, for her part, wanted to represent the Burmese people, even if she did not like the government. She continued as ambassador for a few years. In 1967, however, she resigned, feeling that she could no longer serve as the "face" of a government she despised. With both her children now living abroad, she returned home to 54 University Avenue to live the quiet life of a private citizen. A few old friends of Aung San would come by, but talking about politics was dangerous. Democracy seemed like a distant dream.

Suu Kyi's brother, Aung San Oo, finished his studies in England and moved to the United States to study engineering. He would eventually become a US citizen and break with Myanmar almost completely. He had no interest in his native land. Suu Kyi felt trapped between two worlds. She loved the freedom of living abroad but could not forget her heritage. She had no future in Myanmar, but neither could she leave it behind.

FREEDOM TO LEAD

Aung San Suu Kyi became a powerful symbol of the prodemocracy movement in Myanmar in the 1990s.

CHAPTER THREE

The Path to Leadership

S uu Kyi's path to leadership would take many slow and winding turns between 1965 and 1988. While her country suffered under the heel of tyranny, she would puzzle out just what her duty to that country was and how she might someday fulfill it.

The 1960s were known as a revolutionary decade. Throughout Europe and the United States, young people in search of freedom defied authority. Blue jeans replaced tailored suits and dresses on college campuses. Rock and roll blared from radios and stereo speakers. The Beatles, the Rolling Stones, Janis Joplin, Bob Dylan, and Jimi Hendrix provided the soundtrack for protests and demonstrations.

The US war in Vietnam became a flash point for protests both in America and abroad. "The times," as Bob Dylan sang, "they are a-changin."

Yet Suu Kyi stood back from the uproar. At St. Hugh's College in Oxford, England, she appeared different and slightly quaint in her traditional *aingyi* and *longyi*. She had little interest in parties. Once, curious as to why her fellow students liked drinking alcohol so much, she purchased a small bottle, took a few swigs, and then poured the contents down the drain. Liquor tasted strange and sour to her. Her mother never drank it, and Suu Kyi decided then and there that neither would she. Because she assumed she would marry a fellow countryman, she rarely dated. She preferred classical to pop tunes. Still, she made several close friends, among them Anne Pasternak Slater, the niece of the Russian poet and novelist Boris Pasternak. Suu Kyi taught Anne how to eat rice with her fingers, Burmese style, and how to wear a *longyi*. Pasternak Slater encouraged Suu Kyi to loosen up a bit. Taking the hint, Suu Kyi bought a pair of jeans (white, not blue) and learned how to ride a bicycle and steer a flat-bottomed raft called a punt along Oxford's river. Even barefoot in jeans, she impressed people with her poise and grace. She knew how to listen, and her early experience with loss made her sensitive to other people's troubles. One of her professors remembered her as "a wholly composed, self-aware young woman."

Deep inside, however, Suu Kyi was not quite so composed. She had arrived at St. Hugh's in 1965 to pursue a degree in politics, philosophy, and economics, otherwise known in Oxford as PPE. Her courses, though, seemed dry and boring. She would have preferred to switch her major to literature, but the college would not allow it. As a result, her studies suffered. She passed, but without high grades. A friend recalled that she was deeply interested in the ideas of nonviolence presented by Gandhi. Whenever the topic of conversation turned to Myanmar, she spoke of her father and her own desire to make a difference, to contribute something to her country. She didn't know how to act on this ambition, though. She didn't see herself as someone who could wield power and certainly not as someone who could lead an uprising. Returning to Myanmar while Ne Win controlled the government was dangerous. She knew from her mother that protests had been put down by force. She had no future back home.

A Time of Transition

After receiving her degree in 1967, she took a job as a research assistant for a professor of Asian studies at London University. She spent most of her weekends with her friends the Gore-Booths. They had twin sons close in age to Suu Kyi, and their house always seemed to be filled with a lively crowd of young people. One afternoon, she was introduced to another set of twins, Michael and Anthony Aris. Michael was immediately drawn to Suu Kyi because since childhood he had been fascinated by Tibetan Buddhism. Like Suu Kyi, he was introverted, a listener rather than a talker. Together, though, they had a lot to share. Suu Kyi was charmed by this Englishman who had learned so much about her Buddhist culture. To everyone who knew them, it was obvious they were falling in love.

Suu Kyi, however, didn't want to make a commitment. Aris was a year younger than she was. She dreaded telling her mother she was even thinking of marrying a foreigner. Besides, they were both headed in opposite directions. Suu Kyi had received an invitation to live in New York, one she felt she could not turn down. Aris, meanwhile, had been offered a position as tutor to the royal family of Bhutan in the Himalaya Mountains, one of the world's most remote countries. All they could do was promise to write to one another and see how well their love could endure.

In New York, Suu Kyi took courses at New York University and worked in an administrative office at the United Nations. She lived with Ma Than E, an old family friend. Ma Than E also worked at the United Nations and introduced Suu Kyi to U Thant, the UN's secretary-general and possibly the most famous Burmese person in the world after he had been named to his post by the UN's member nations in 1961. U Thant was the first non-European to lead the organization. Although Myanmar was a dictatorship, U Thant was almost universally admired as a fair and just man. He had known Aung San and was happy to help the Bogyoke's daughter feel at home in New York. Suu Kyi and Ma Than E went to many parties given by U Thant and the head of the Burmese delegation, U Soe Tin.

One of those parties left Suu Kyi with a bitter taste in her mouth. She arrived at Soe Tin's house to find herself

U Thant of Myanmar served as secretary-general of the United Nations from 1961 to 1971. He was the first non-European to hold the office.

surrounded by Burmese officials. They demanded to know why she was still using the diplomatic passport she had received when her mother was ambassador to India. The question puzzled Suu Kyi. She had applied for a regular Burmese passport, she told them, but had not yet received it. The paperwork had been delayed, that was all. Then she realized that Ne Win must have learned that Aung San's daughter was working at the UN and wondered if she was trying to pass herself off as the "official" Burmese representative and take over the delegation. The idea seemed ridiculous to Suu Kyi. She had no such intention, she assured the officials. She was amazed that Ne Win would even consider her a threat—she didn't have any power. She wasn't interested in politics; all she wanted to do was help her country. The officials backed down, but Ne Win continued to keep his eye on the Bogyoke's daughter.

Love and Duty

Over the course of three years, Suu Kyi and Michael Aris exchanged 187 letters. He never wavered in his commitment to her. Finally, she said yes. Suu Kyi quit her job at the UN, and Aris took a break from his work in Bhutan to fly back to England. On January 2, 1972, they were married in a small ceremony at the Gore-Booths' house. A Buddhist monk performed the ritual, winding a white string, which symbolized spiritual connection,

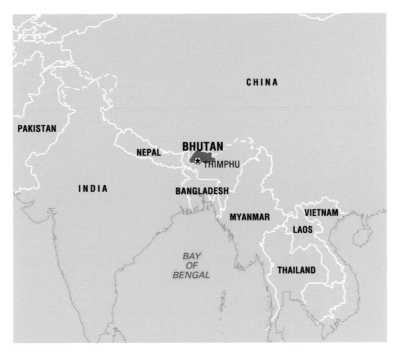

The Kingdom of Bhutan is located in the eastern Himalaya Mountains. Its government is a constitutional monarchy.

around the bride and groom. Neither Suu Kyi's brother nor her mother attended, though she had invited them both. If she was disappointed, she didn't show it. The few friends who came remembered her as a radiant bride.

Soon after the wedding, Suu Kyi returned with Aris to Bhutan. Although the people were Buddhist, certain aspects of their culture were strange to her. Bhutan was ruled by a king; commoners, including Aris and herself, were expected to bow whenever a member of the royal family passed by. This annoyed Suu Kyi more than it did Aris. She didn't mind, she said, bowing to the king and queen, but the royal couple seemed to have an endless number of sons, daughters, nephews, nieces, and cousins who all demanded the same show of respect. She looked forward to the times when Aris could get away from his teaching responsibilities at the court. Then they would hike or ride ponies through the mountains, where the only people they encountered were humble villagers who required no bowing.

By late 1972, Aris felt he had finally gathered enough material to start writing his dissertation and finish his degree. Suu Kyi discovered she was pregnant then, too. They returned to England, where she gave birth to a boy they named Alexander in 1973. In 1974, Aris received an offer to work in Nepal. While they were there, Suu Kyi arranged for them to make a brief visit to her mother in Yangon, but she was nervous. Khin Kyi had made no secret of her disapproval. Her daughter had disappointed her greatly by marrying an Englishman. Suu Kyi needn't have worried—the stern Khin Kyi melted at the sight of her grandson. Within a few days, Aris's kindness had won her over, too.

The family returned for another visit a few months later. This time Suu Kyi left Aris and Khin Kyi alone to get to know one another while she explored the streets of her old hometown. The fear she sensed in the people pained her. So many Burmese seemed to have become resigned to tyranny. Those who wanted change had no

Suu Kyi with her two sons, Alexander Aris (*left*) and Kim Aris (*right*), in the late 1970s

leader. When she encountered one of her father's old colleagues, she asked him, "Do you think you have fulfilled your responsibilities to your country?"

"Rest assured I will continue to meet my obligations to the nation," he replied. "But you must do your part."

His words were not lost on her. She still believed she had a part to play in Myanmar's history, but she didn't know what it was. And she couldn't stay in Myanmar; Aris's work was taking him back to England. The family settled in Oxford, where Aris began to teach at the university. Suu Kyi gave birth to a second son, Kim, in 1977.

Aris's salary was not large. Money was tight, and they struggled to make ends meet. Somehow Suu Kyi always found the means to entertain the frequent guests who arrived from America, Bhutan, and Myanmar. No matter how much she had to scrimp and save, she made sure they never turned anyone away. She cooked, cleaned, helped her children with their homework, and took occasional jobs writing or doing research to earn extra money. She was fulfilling her duty to her family, but what of her other duty, she wondered?

News from Myanmar was discouraging. Although Ne Win had officially stepped down as prime minister in 1974, he remained the head of his party and the most powerful figure in Myanmar. In the 1980s, his behavior became unpredictable and even bizarre. When an astrologer told him that nine was his lucky number, he canceled all of Myanmar's currency and insisted that money be reissued in increments of nine. Everyone's old money became worthless, and the country was thrown into economic chaos. Foreign investors avoided Myanmar. Foreign governments kept contact to a minimum, and the country became isolated from the larger world.

Suu Kyi tried to visit her mother every summer near Martyr's Day on July 19. As her sons became older, she brought them with her so they could learn about their Burmese heritage. She could not imagine moving to Myanmar permanently, though. Instead, she thought she might fulfill her duty to her nation by becoming a scholar of its history and literature. She applied to several graduate programs in England. In 1985, she received a fellowship to spend a year in Japan. She wanted to learn more about her father's relationship to that country through the archives and records there.

Suu Kyi took her younger son, Kim, with her to Kyoto, Japan. Aris and their older son, Alexander, went to the Indian Himalayas, where Aris would do research for a year. In Japan, Suu Kyi immersed herself in the study of her father's life. A Japanese friend noted that Burmese exchange students attending Kyoto University regarded Suu Kyi with a respect that bordered on awe. They were far too young to remember Aung San, but they knew about him. Nobody in Myanmar had forgotten the Bogyoke. His daughter was the closest they could come to his legend. Their regard both pleased and intimidated Suu Kyi. She didn't know what they expected of her. The more she studied her father, the closer she began to feel to her country. They were, she once told an interviewer, nearly one and the same.

In 1986, the family returned to England. Now that her sons were becoming independent, Suu Kyi hoped to devote herself to writing. Perhaps she could produce a scholarly book on Myanmar. Feeling that she was at last on the right path, Suu Kyi began to work toward a doctoral degree in Burmese literature. She never completed it. Two years later, her life took a completely different turn.

Into the Storm

On March 31, 1988, Suu Kyi received a call telling her that her mother had had a stroke. That same month, Myanmar finally reached its breaking point. The economy was collapsing. Once more, people discovered their money was worthless. Food became scarce. Businesses closed. The UN labeled Myanmar one of the world's "least developed nations." The country that had once been the "rice basket" of Asia was now among the poorest of the poor.

In mid-March, students at Yangon University had staged anti-government protests. The police had opened fire, killing hundreds. The exact number was not known because the army had disposed of the bodies before they could be identified. Other students died after they were arrested. At least forty suffocated when they were crammed into the back of a van built to hold only a half-dozen people. The government closed the university and ordered

Suu Kyi addresses a prodemocracy rally at the Shwedagon Pagoda in Yangon on August 26, 1988.

the teashops where students gathered to shut their doors. The city's economic and social life came to a standstill.

When Suu Kyi arrived in Yangon, she went directly to the hospital where her mother was a patient. She could not help noticing the injured young people that filled the wards. After she made her mother comfortable, she went out to talk to them. They told her how specially trained cadres of riot police, called Lon Htein, had shot, stabbed, clubbed, strangled, and drowned peaceful demonstrators as they attempted to cross the White Bridge, a narrow path that passed along Inya Lake. The White Bridge Massacre signaled the beginning of the 1988 Uprising, a revolt that would change Myanmar forever.

Over the next few months, Suu Kyi stayed with her mother in the hospital and listened to the students. Those who recovered were replaced by those recently released from prison. They told Suu Kyi about beatings and torture, about people thrown into cells and left without food or water for days, about the screams that echoed down the prison's corridors at night. The ones that were freed considered themselves lucky. Many of their friends remained behind. Suu Kyi said little but thought a lot. She knew that the enemy was not just the army or police; it was violence itself. How could protesters confront violence without becoming violent, she wondered. It was easy to talk about nonviolence but hard to put it into action.

Suu Kyi's first concern, however, was for her mother. When it became clear that the hospital doctors could do nothing for her, Suu Kyi took her home to 54 University Avenue, hoping that she might die there in peace. She asked Aris to come with their sons, so they could say goodbye. But the house was far from peaceful. It was as if a dam had broken in the city. Suddenly everyone wanted to talk politics, and the house of Aung San's widow seemed the best place to do it. Old friends and colleagues of Khin Kyi came by to discuss the recent events, along with students and young people who had heard about Suu Kyi or met her in the hospital.

Khin Kyi was probably less upset by the stream of visitors than her daughter. Like her husband, she believed that politics was life. Each and every person was political in some way. Khin Kyi concentrated on spending her remaining time with her grandsons; their presence made her feel stronger. She was in no danger of dying immediately, she told Suu Kyi. She encouraged Suu Kyi to spend her time talking with those who gathered at the house.

On July 23, Ne Win announced that he was stepping down to allow for democratic elections. Two weeks later, on August 8, 1988, people staged massive prodemocracy demonstrations throughout the nation. At least ten thousand of them converged on Yangon. For the most part the demonstrators remained peaceful. Many carried signs with pictures of Aung San. Others waved flags with images of the peacock, Myanmar's ancient symbol of prosperity. Soldiers were met with flowers.

All day the demonstrations went on. They began to look more like a celebration or festival. Darkness fell and people remained in the streets, talking, sharing food, and singing the national anthem. At 11:30 p.m., the army struck. Trucks bore down on the demonstrators from all sides. Once they had surrounded them, the soldiers opened fire. An estimated three thousand civilians died in Yangon. Similar armed assaults took place in other locations. Even the protesters who had gathered at sacred temples were not spared.

Suu Kyi was at home with her family and had not participated in the demonstrations. When news of the slaughter reached her, she knew she could not remain silent any longer. She put word out that she would speak from the steps of the Shwedagon Pagoda on August 26, the same place where her father had called for democracy in 1946.

People began arriving at the pagoda on August 25. They brought blankets and camped out all night. A huge poster of Aung San had been erected at the top of the steps where Suu Kyi was to speak. A Burmese reporter estimated that the crowd may have been as high as six hundred thousand. General Ne Win rarely attracted more than two hundred thousand. The army was well aware of the event, but even Ne Win was reluctant to openly confront the Bogyoke's daughter. Perhaps he hoped her speech would be a failure—people would dismiss her as a rich woman spoiled by living abroad, and she would simply go away. If that's what he anticipated, he was soon disappointed.

Suu Kyi arrived at the pagoda with her husband and sons, flanked by unarmed "bodyguards" who were young students. She wore a crisp cotton *aingyi* and *longyi* and a white flower in her hair. After a short introduction from one of Myanmar's most popular film stars, she greeted the crowd: "Reverend monks and people!"

She openly acknowledged that she had spent most of her life abroad and that some might think she knew little about Myanmar. "The trouble is," she pointed out, "I know too much." Reading from carefully prepared notes, she told the audience, "I could not as my father's daughter remain indifferent to all that was going on." She called the protests Myanmar's second struggle for independence. She said she sought to unite the country, not divide it. She wanted the military to answer to a civilian government, as it did in Western democracies. Above all, she urged democracy and free elections.

Much of what she said was plain common sense, yet people applauded wildly. Some applauded because she was the Bogyoke's daughter, but many more genuinely liked what she had to say. "She spoke elegantly but simply," one listener recalled, "so that everyone could understand what she meant." People were tired of military leaders. They trusted this woman with her firm, clear voice, who told them that democracy was the only form of government that "promotes and strengthens peace."

The government responded to Suu Kyi's speech with a massive crackdown on September 18. For four days, the military took over cities, towns, and villages, firing upon almost any group of civilians large or small. When it was over, an estimated ten thousand people had died.

Ne Win formed the State Law and Order Restoration Council (SLORC) and imposed martial law. All public assemblies of more than four persons were banned.

On September 24, Suu Kyi and a small group of supporters formed the National League for Democracy (NLD), a political party based on nonviolence and **civil disobedience**. Suu Kyi became the new party's secretary-general. Her sons had already gone back to school in England, and soon Aris would be leaving to go back to work. There was no question of what Suu Kyi would do. She had promised her people she would stay for as long as it took to create a true democracy.

The Prisoner

In the space of six months, Suu Kyi had gone from a mild-mannered housewife to the leader of the largest opposition party in one of the most repressive countries in the world. The government had promised free elections but forbid campaigning. Suu Kyi decided to campaign anyway. From October 1988 to July 1989, she toured the nation, stopping at towns and villages everywhere. Her campaign was interrupted only by her mother's funeral in January 1989. Aris and her sons returned for the funeral and left shortly after. Her brother came too, but they had little to say to one another. Aung San Oo did not approve of her politics, and the two siblings eventually became completely estranged.

Prodemocracy activists held demonstrations throughout Myanmar during the uprising of 1988.

Without her mother, Suu Kyi must have felt terribly alone in Myanmar. She was surrounded by loyal supporters yet had few people she could call close friends. She looked forward to the summer, when her family could come and visit her again. They had promised to return for Martyr's Day in July.

The government had other plans for Suu Kyi. Her famous confrontation in Danubyu was the last straw. Ne Win wanted to get rid of her. He knew he couldn't kill her without causing a major uproar. Putting her in jail would have the same effect. He couldn't kidnap her or make her disappear without triggering more protests. So he decided to hide her in plain sight: she would become the woman

MAHATMA GANDHI

Born to a Hindu family in India in 1869, Mahatma Gandhi is considered the father of modern nonviolent movements. He led the Indian rebellion against British rule using boycotts, civil disobedience, passive resistance, fasting, and other peaceful strategies. He had developed his philosophy of nonviolence while working as a young lawyer in South Africa, where the policy of

apartheid enforced a rigid separation of ethnic groups. One day, a European asked Gandhi to give up his seat on a train. When he peacefully refused, the conductor threw him off at the next station. The experience changed his life. In 1906, he organized a nonviolent protest against laws that restricted the rights of Indians in South Africa and won important concessions from the government, granting Indians more freedom.

Gandhi promoted a concept he called Satyagraha, Hindi for "Truth and Firmness." When he returned to India, he joined the Indian independence movement and staged his most famous campaign, the Salt March of 1930. Britain had imposed a large tax on salt and forbade the Indians from obtaining natural salt from seawater. Over sixty thousand people followed Gandhi on a march across India to the sea, where they harvested salt from the ocean in direct defiance of the law. The British imprisoned Gandhi for his efforts, but his movement could not be stopped.

Britain withdrew from India in 1946. Gandhi feared a civil war would erupt between Muslims and Hindus and tried to negotiate peace between the two groups, but he was assassinated by a Hindu nationalist in 1948. Gandhi's ideas have inspired Martin Luther King, Nelson Mandela, Aung San Suu Kyi, and many other nonviolent protesters throughout the world.

who wasn't there. Everyone would know where she was. She would be right at home until people forgot that she existed and she didn't matter anymore.

Alexander and Kim arrived in Myanmar, as they had planned, in mid-July 1989. Aris had been delayed in Scotland and would join them later. On the morning of July 20, Suu Kyi awoke to find the street in front of her house blocked off by soldiers. In addition to her sons, about forty students were also staying in the compound. She told them to leave by the back entrance. Some made it home, but most were arrested and taken away. Around four in the afternoon, a soldier knocked on the door. When Suu Kyi answered, he told her that she was under house arrest. Guards would be stationed around her property. She would not be allowed to leave her house or receive any visitors without government permission. Then several soldiers entered and searched the house, opening draws and closets, taking paper away by the armload. Suu Kyi was not frightened. Alexander and Kim were safe. The soldiers were not violent.

The students who had been arrested, however, were not so fortunate. They had been taken to Insein Prison. Insein was notorious for its brutal guards and routine use of torture. Suu Kyi announced that she would not eat until she received a guarantee the students would not be tortured or harmed in any way. When Aris arrived three days later, he found her lying on her bed, hollow eyed and weak. Alexander and Kim were alarmed, but Suu Kyi remained calm. She explained her actions to her husband, and Aris asked the government about the fate of the students, but the officials ignored him. For a week, Suu Kyi refused to eat. News of her hunger strike leaked out to the people and the press; she grew weaker. Aris pointed out to the government that they did not want a martyr on their hands. After twelve days, Suu Kyi had lost a tenth of her body weight. She could no longer get out of bed. No amount of pleading could make her eat. Finally, the government gave in and promised her that the students would not be abused.

The government told her she was free to return to England with her husband and children. That should have been good news. It wasn't. Suu Kyi knew that if she left, she would never be allowed to return. Her Burmese passport would be revoked. Ne Win could have deported her by force, but he didn't want her to be a victim pushed into exile. He wanted people to see her leave of her own free will. He wanted them to believe that she just didn't care about Myanmar after all. She preferred a comfortable life back in Britain, like any other wealthy lady. Campaigning for democracy had only been a pastime, a game to her. Suu Kyi refused. If this was a battle of wills, she was going to win. The Burmese government wanted people to forget about her. Instead, they made her the most famous prisoner in the world.

After her release from house arrest in 1995, Suu Kyi held "free speech meetings" for supporters who gathered outside the gates of her home at 54 University Avenue in Yangon.

CHAPTER FOUR

The Long Fight for Freedom

S hut away from the world behind the gates of 54 University Avenue, Suu Kyi set about building a life. All the self-discipline her mother had taught her came to her aid now. She rose every morning by 4:30 a.m. and meditated for an hour. Suu Kyi was a naturally busy person, and she did not find sitting still easy, but gradually she learned to calm her mind. She discovered when she meditated she did not feel afraid. "It is not power that corrupts," she wrote, "but fear." She did not want to be corrupted by fear.

After meditating, she would eat breakfast and listen to the news on the radio. The soldiers had let her keep her radio, and it served as her one precious link to the outside world. She had a small library of books, mostly on history and Buddhism, and she set aside a few hours each day for reading and writing. She had a piano and could play for hours on end. When things got too much for her, however, she would take her anger out on the keys, banging her way through the music until the instrument was sadly out of tune. Only the piano experienced her rage. People rarely got a glimpse of what she felt inside.

She kept her clothes clean and pressed, and she greeted the guards as if they were visitors, not jailers. In return, the soldiers treated her politely. A few of the younger ones asked if she would teach them a bit of English. She enjoyed that but noticed if she got too close to any of her guards they would be quickly replaced.

She was not entirely alone. The house was more like an estate, with several smaller buildings around it. At various times, three or four female companions lived there with her, including her aunt. They helped Suu Kyi cook and clean and maintain the house, which was old and leaked when it rained. She did not want to become too dependent on them, though, for they might be punished for helping her too much.

A Lonely and Difficult Life

After her sons returned to England in September 1989, Myanmar revoked their visas. Without visas, they could not return—it would be years before she would see them again. Her husband came alone that Christmas and drew out the holiday by giving her one gift a day over a period of twelve days. On a certain level, her life seemed peaceful and calm. But the knowledge that others suffered because of their connection with her ate away at her soul.

She refused to let the government provide her with food. Instead, she asked the guards to sell her possessions and buy provisions with the money they received. She gave up her jewelry, artwork, vases, woven rugs, and all the furnishings her mother had collected over the years. She ate sparingly, her bones became fragile, her back often hurt, and she had a weak heart. Yet she never forgot that others were far worse off. To keep up her spirits, she copied quotes and sayings from Gandhi and hung them on the walls to remind herself what she was fighting for.

The government allowed Aris to send her packages, but when they photographed the contents and splashed the pictures across the front page of the newspaper, Suu Kyi refused to accept the gifts anymore. She had only asked for a few ordinary things—paperback mystery novels, hand cream, a recent issue of a magazine—but taken together, these small items represented unimaginable riches to many of Myanmar's citizens. The government publicized them to embarrass her, to make it look as if she were an aristocrat being waited on hand and foot. That was the last impression she wanted to give. She had to be very careful in her dealings with the authorities.

In the spring of 1990, the military junta announced that elections would be held. The generals were so confident the NLD had been completely crushed that they even let Suu Kyi cast a ballot. On May 27, the results came in. The NLD had won 392 of 492 seats in the assembly, an astounding victory. The government immediately announced that the election didn't count. Saw Maung, the chairman of the SLORC, remained the prime minister, though he had won no votes. Suu Kyi might have been frustrated, but she refused to give up hope. The election was proof that people wanted democracy, even if the generals did not.

The Lady at the Gate

In Yangon, the street that passed Suu Kyi's house was so well guarded that few people could get a glimpse of her. In the outside world, however, she was about to become famous. In July 1991, the European Parliament awarded her the Sakharov Prize for Freedom of Thought. Three months later, on October 14, she received the Nobel Peace Prize, one of the world's highest honors. The Nobel

Michael Aris and sons, Alexander and Kim, accepted the Nobel Peace Prize on Suu Kyi's behalf while she was under house arrest in 1991.

Committee could not call her with the news, so they contacted Michael Aris, who was teaching at Harvard University in the United States. "Many will now for the first time learn of [Suu Kyi's] courageous leadership of the nonviolent struggle for the restoration of human rights in her country," he told the press. He added that the joy he and his sons felt was matched by their concern. The government had cut off all contact with Suu Kyi by mail or phone. At that moment, her husband did not know if she was alive or dead.

Saw Maung and his generals were furious to find they had an international celebrity on their hands. After they grudgingly admitted that yes, she was still alive and still under house arrest, requests from the media began to pour in. Everyone wanted to know more about the mysterious woman with the flower in her hair. What had she done, they asked, that made a group of armed men so afraid they had to lock her behind her own gate?

Suu Kyi heard bits and pieces of this on her radio. She was amused and a bit embarrassed. She only accepted the awards for her people, she insisted, not for herself. Aris used the Nobel Prize money to set up a fund for Myanmar. Though she may have been selling her last tables and chairs to get by, she didn't want to keep any of the prize money for herself.

Over the next few years, power shifted in the government from one general to another. The junta wanted to improve Myanmar's international image and attract more foreign investment. That was hard to do when they were holding a Nobel Prize winner captive. On July 10, 1995, Yangon's chief of police knocked on Suu Kyi's door and told her she was free. She had not stepped beyond her front gate in six years.

Suu Kyi knew that most people in Myanmar did not have access to international media. She might have been

Suu Kyi often spoke about nonviolence and civil rights to the crowds that assembled outside her gates in the mid-1990s.

famous abroad, but would all those ordinary people who struggled to earn a living every day at home remember her? They did. Within hours, the street outside her house was packed with well-wishers. She didn't know what else to say except, "Hello, how are you?" as she reached through the fence to touch their hands.

People came back the next day and the day after that. Someone brought a table from the house so Suu Kyi could stand on it and talk to the crowd over the fence.

Soon her daily talks at her gate became a major event in Yangon. People came by the thousands. Vendors hawked food. TV and radio stations came with trucks. Suu Kyi felt flattered but overwhelmed. She could not talk to the crowd every day, so she set up a schedule of "free speech" meetings on Saturday and Sunday afternoons at her front gate. For an hour, she took questions and explained basic concepts of democracy, such as freedom of the press and fair elections. A visiting reporter from the *New York Times* noted that she sometimes talked about Martin Luther King.

Suu Kyi's message remained consistent: nonviolence was the only way to achieve democracy. As she told the journalist Alan Clements:

Nonviolence means positive action. You have to work for whatever you want. You don't just sit there doing nothing and hope to get what you want. It just means that the methods you use are not violent ones. Some people think that nonviolence is passiveness. It is not so.

For Suu Kyi, taking action meant taking up the campaign for democracy again. Once more, 54 University Avenue became a hub of political activity. She was grateful to discover that many of the possessions she had sold had actually been stored in a warehouse for her by sympathetic guards. She insisted on paying them back with the money she earned from her book *Freedom from Fear*, a collection of essays by and about her that Aris had compiled in 1991.

An Uneasy Freedom

Suu Kyi used her own newfound freedom to criticize the government's attempts to attract tourists to Myanmar. All the shiny new hotels and resorts did not raise the standard of living for ordinary people, she said. Economic development meant nothing without human rights.

The government's response was to teach her just how limited her freedom actually was. Blockades would suddenly appear on her street. Her phone line would go dead. Friends and supporters would be taken in for questioning by the police after visiting her. When she and other members of the NLD tried to leave Yangon to speak to people in the countryside, army vehicles blockaded her car. The soldiers would order her to go back, but Suu Kyi and her colleagues would refuse. The standoff might go on for days. Once Suu Kyi sat trapped in her car for eleven days, subsisting on meager bites of food and sips of water, until she finally fainted and had to be taken home in an ambulance. She insisted she was not trying to be a martyr; she just believed she and every other Burmese citizen had the right to travel around the country freely.

Michael Aris (1946–1999), scholar and college professor, wrote several books on Buddhism.

Paying an Unimaginable Price

Then, in 1999, Suu Kyi received the worst possible news. Michael Aris had cancer, and he was dying. He wanted to come to Myanmar, but the government refused to let him in. Suu Kyi could fly to England to be with him, but she knew she would never be allowed to return. She did not go. It was the hardest decision she ever made. Aris understood; they would be together in spirit, he said.

Michael Aris died on March 27, 1999, at the age of fifty-three. Suu Kyi had chosen to put her duty to her country first, and she had paid the highest possible price. She did not regret it—the only way to honor Aris's memory was to continue with her work.

On May 30, 2003, Suu Kyi would almost lose her own life. Armed gangs attacked her convoy of cars on the road to the town of Depayin. They pulled people from the vehicles and beat them to death with clubs. Seventy of her supporters died. Suu Kyi believed the attackers had been hired by the government. She escaped only because her quick-thinking driver stamped his foot on the gas pedal and plowed through the roadblock. Later that night, she was arrested and sent to Insein Prison. She stayed there for three months before being placed under house arrest again.

For the next seven years, she would remain at home, a prisoner behind her own gate. This third sentence (she had served a second house arrest term from 2000 to 2002) was both a defeat and a victory. It was a defeat because it clearly showed that Myanmar was not a democracy and all her efforts had gotten it no closer to that goal. But it was a victory because, once more, the government still had no idea what to do about her. She would not go away. Despite all their attempts to silence her, she would not be quiet. She would not disappear.

Suu Kyi was now the world's most famous **prisoner of conscience**. First Ladies Hillary Clinton and Laura Bush spoke on her behalf when they lived in the White House. President Bill Clinton awarded her the Presidential Medal of Freedom in 2000. President George W. Bush gave her a Congressional Gold Medal in 2008. The list of her prizes and medals could go on for pages. They include the International Simón Bolívar Prize (1992), the Jawaharlal Nehru Award for International Understanding (1993), the Wallenberg Medal (2011), the Olof Palme Prize (2005), and even the MTV Europe Free Your Mind Award (2003).

Suu Kyi received many international distinctions. In 2012, she became an honorary citizen of the city of Paris.

The Saffron Revolution

While Suu Kyi was under house arrest, Myanmar's government began to change. International pressure on the military junta increased. The United States and other Western powers maintained **sanctions** against Myanmar, limiting trade and preventing Myanmar from joining international organizations and alliances. These sanctions would only be lifted if the junta granted Myanmar's citizens their rights.

In 2007, Myanmar's monks became involved in the prodemocracy movement, staging demonstrations that riveted the attention of the world. Monks have always had a special place in Myanmar's culture. They are seen as the protectors and preservers of Buddhist traditions. Monasteries are centers of learning, and monastery schools have provided education for Myanmar's children for thousands of years. People often turn to monks for guidance in their personal lives or advice in settling small legal disputes. Even non-Buddhists tend to regard the Buddhist monks with respect. Buddhist monks earn their living by begging in the streets, but this is not looked down upon. Among Buddhists, giving to a monk is seen as a way of acquiring spiritual benefits. The presence of monks in the streets collecting coins serves as a constant reminder of the connection between the material and spiritual world.

In 2007, thousands of Burmese monks took part in anti-government demonstrations that became known as the Saffron Revolution.

For the most part, monks are not political. Though some had joined prodemocracy demonstrations, they did so as individuals, not as a group. In 2007, three monks were injured when the army broke up a demonstration against rising fuel prices in the province of Pokokku. In a startling move of retaliation, local monks took three government officials hostage and demanded the government apologize. The government refused. The monks responded by refusing to provide religious services to members of the military and their families. When soldiers tried to give money to begging monks, the monks would turn their bowls upside down. Refusing a donation is considered a grave insult to the donor, for it is also a way of denying that person spiritual benefits. The monks were saying that those who worked for the government were not worthy of spiritual salvation.

Thousands of monks began to join the protests. They were not just protesting the treatment of their fellow monks at Pokokku, but also the poverty and misery they saw all around them. The Burmese economy was in yet another crisis. The cost of basic necessities such as fuel and food had risen as much as 500 percent in some regions; even monks could no longer remain silent.

On September 2, Suu Kyi was awakened by a commotion in the street outside her house. Chants of *Myitta Thote*, the Buddhist phrase for "loving kindness," echoed through the air. When she went to her door, she saw hundreds of monks in their dark-red robes gathered in front of her gate. They had marched right over the barricades that blocked off the avenue. With tears streaming down her face, she rushed to the fence and reached through the bars to grasp their hands. *Myitta Thote, Myitta Thote*, she whispered. It was the first time she had been seen outside her house by members of the public in almost four years.

The protesting monks' movement became known as the Saffron Revolution, after the color of their robes, though Burmese monks wear red rather than the saffron orange of monks in other countries. At first, the government did not know what to do about the demonstrations. Attacking large groups of peaceful monks seemed too much even for the junta. The government imposed curfews, but the monks refused to shut down their protests after dark. Ordinary people came out to protect the monks, forming a human shield around them as they marched through the streets.

The government retaliated by raiding monasteries, dragging monks out, and hauling them away to prison. They attacked the protesters, injuring and killing monks and civilians alike. All these incidents were captured on cell phones and digital cameras and broadcast to the rest of the world. People across the globe were horrified. Something would have to change.

Politics and Power

Even under house arrest, Suu Kyi remained the leader of the opposition to Myanmar's government. In September 2009, Hillary Clinton, who was then US secretary of state, met with Burmese officials. She told them the US government would lift its sanctions if Myanmar would free Suu Kyi and hold democratic elections. In November 2010, Suu Kyi was finally freed from house arrest. The government also gave her permission to have an internet connection. For the first time, she could talk directly with the world.

President Barack Obama met with Suu Kyi during his tour of Asia in November 2012.

In 2011, the military junta stepped down. Thein Sein became president of Myanmar's first civilian government. He declared that the government would allow people to participate in peaceful demonstrations and promised that free elections would be held in 2012.

With all her awards and admirers, it would be easy to understand why Suu Kyi might want to take it easy after her release from house arrest. She was sixty-five years old and had spent almost seventeen of the last twenty-one years of her life in one form of detention or another. Her sons were grown men with children of their own. She wanted to reconnect and get to know them again, and she was now free to leave Myanmar and return. If she wished to, she could travel the world, giving speeches and earning thousands of dollars in speaker's fees.

Instead, she announced that she would run for public office. She had committed herself to helping Myanmar become a democracy. If she could help Myanmar by holding pubic office, that's what she would do. In 2012, she ran for an open seat in the parliament as a member of the NLD and won.

Her election, however, coincided with a crisis in human rights that would cast a shadow over her success and raise some serious questions about her true ambitions.

The Rohingya Crisis

The Rohingya are a Muslim minority in Myanmar who live in the Rakhine state, a narrow strip of land along Myanmar's coast. Most of them occupy a small peninsula that borders on Bangladesh. Rohingya people have lived in the region for hundreds of years; for most of that history, the relations between the Rohingya and the Buddhists remained peaceful. After Myanmar gained independence from Britain, however, tensions between the two groups emerged. As Muslims, the Rohingya feared they would

In the early twenty-first century, many Rohingya have been forced to flee Myanmar for refugee camps in Thailand and Bangladesh.

lose their rights under a Buddhist-majority government. Many Buddhists believed that Muslims were still loyal to Britain and would not be good citizens of the new country. To avoid persecution, thousands of Rohingya fled across the border to Bangladesh. Some Rohingya wanted to establish an independent state and staged a small rebellion, which the government quickly put down. The rebellion never had the support of most Rohingya and was not a major threat to the stability of the state, but it became an excuse for the government to seize Rohingya land and deny them rights. Under the military junta, many Rohingya were declared noncitizens and were forbidden from holding government jobs. When the Rohingya protested, they were beaten, arrested, forced into exile, or killed.

In 2012, tensions between the Muslim Rohingya and the Buddhist majority in Rakhine exploded in a series of violent conflicts that left over a hundred dead. Thousands of Rohingya became refugees, fleeing to camps in Thailand. The Rohingya accused the government of arming the Buddhists and encouraging their assaults upon Rohingya villages. The government denied the charges, but its treatment of the Rohingya raised international concern. Human rights groups accused Myanmar of engaging in a campaign of **ethnic cleansing** to force the Rohingya from the country entirely.

Many people expected Suu Kyi to speak out on behalf of the Rohingya. They felt that she had a duty as Myanmar's most famous advocate of human rights to protest against the persecution of any minority. But Suu Kyi remained silent. When pressed for her views, she only replied that there had been violence on both sides. This attitude alarmed even her most loyal international supporters. What she said was true, but the Rohingya were far more likely to be victims of violence than the Buddhists were. Human rights activists began to wonder if Suu Kyi had abandoned her principles now that she was part of the government. One group even started an online campaign recall her Nobel Peace Prize, saying that she no longer deserved that honor.

Suu Kyi responded that she could not help the cause of democracy in Myanmar by taking sides. Her critics accused her of turning a blind eye to violations of human rights. It was one thing to be fair, they said, but quite another to ignore atrocities. It seemed that Suu Kyi had gone from being one of the most admired women in the world to one of the most despised. She was no longer the heroic lady with the flower in her hair, but an ordinary politician who was more concerned with her own position than she was with the well being of her people. Suu Kyi continued to insist that she cared about the Rohingya as she did about all Myanmar's people. She didn't deny that she had become a politician. Her father, she pointed out, had been a politician, too. Political power, she believed, could be used for good as well as evil. Nevertheless, Suu Kyi had faced her first test as an elected official, and in the eyes of many people, she had failed.

The Leader of Her Country

Despite her troubles with the Rohingya crisis, most of Suu Kyi's supporters in Myanmar remained loyal to her. In 2014, she ran for and won reelection. Her party received

In 2000, the Irish rock band U2 received Dublin's Freedom of the City Award. The award is given to those who have made a major contribution to human rights. U2, headed by the musician Bono (born Paul David Hewson), is known for its work raising funds for victims of famine in Africa and its support for refugees. The other

Musician, composer, and human rights activist Bono wrote a popular song, "Walk On," in Suu Kyi's honor in 2001. He is shown here with Suu Kyi's younger son, Kim Aris.

award winner, Aung San Suu Kyi, was not present. Bono had never heard of Suu Kyi. After learning why she could not come to the award ceremony, he composed a song about her entitled "Walk On." Bono said that the song was "about doing what's right even when your heart tells you otherwise."

Released in February 2001, "Walk On" became one of the top twenty-five singles in the United States that year and reached number one on the record charts in Canada. The song was also included on the album *All That You Can't Leave Behind*. Not surprisingly, the album was banned in Myanmar. Anyone caught with a copy could receive a prison sentence of up to twenty years.

When the band played the song in live concerts, they sometimes invited fans to come onto the stage and walk in a circle carrying posters of Suu Kyi. The song also served as an anthem for all those in crises. On September 21, 2001, U2 performed "Walk On" at a televised benefit concert for the families of the firemen who had died in the 9/11 terrorist attacks on the World Trade Center in New York City. In 2012, the song was featured in Amnesty International's Electric Burma Concert, which was organized to raise money for Myanmar and to honor Suu Kyi.

a majority of seats in the parliament and formed a new government. Because of a previous law forbidding those who had married a foreigner from becoming president, Suu Kyi could not hold the highest office. President Htin Kyaw, however, named her state counselor and foreign minister. These posts essentially made her the most powerful person in the government. In April of 2016, she met with President Barack Obama, who called her "a beacon of hope for the entire world."

Problems with the government's treatment of ethnic minorities continued. When questioned by the press, Suu Kyi denied that Myanmar was engaged in a program of ethnic cleansing against the Rohingya. Even many Burmese who had voted for her began to doubt whether she could lead the country. In order to remain in power, she could not rely on the votes of the Buddhist majority alone. The government needed the support of minorities, too, or the country could easily slide into a state of civil war. As the election of 2017 approached, observers began to wonder if Suu Kyi could retain her position. Suu Kyi herself admitted that the new government had failed to live up to its promise. "But," she pointed, "a year is not a long time" in which to create long-term change. Critics charged that she had proved herself incapable of true leadership. She had failed to defend human rights and could not bring order to civil unrest. Her supporters acknowledged her mistakes but believed that replacing her would only lead to greater repression of human rights and undermine the new democracy.

On April 1, 2017, Burmese went to the polls. Suu Kyi's party won half of the open seats, retaining its majority in the parliament. For the time being, her position was

In 2012, Suu Kyi addressed in UN's International Labor Organization in Geneva, Switzerland. She was later criticized by the UN for Myanmar's treatment of its Muslim minorities.

safe. Most of the pro-NLD votes, though, had come from ethnic Buddhists. Few of Myanmar's minorities voted for the party, leading to questions of how well Suu Kyi's government could maintain stability.

In an interview with a reporter from the BBC on April 6, Suu Kyi once more denied that the Rohingya were victims of ethnic cleansing. Those that fled the country, she insisted, would be welcomed back. Human rights activists from the UN and other organizations responded that Muslims in Myanmar had little protection from harassment and assault. They doubted that returning refugees would find any kind of welcome in their former homeland.

Whether Suu Kyi will be remembered as a hero of the human rights movement or as one of its greatest traitors remains to be seen. In her essay "Freedom from Fear," she wrote:

> *Saints, it has been said, are the sinners who go on trying. So free men are the oppressed who go on trying and who in the process make themselves fit to bear the responsibilities and to uphold the disciplines which will maintain a free society.*

Aung San Suu Kyi has made it clear that she intends to go on trying.

CHRONOLOGY

June 19, 1945	Aung San Suu Kyi is born in Yangon, Myanmar.
July 19, 1947	Aung San, father of Suu Kyi, is assassinated.
January 4, 1948	Myanmar gains independence from Britain.
1960–1964	Aung San Suu Kyi attends high school and college in India.
1962	Myanmar becomes a military dictatorship under General Ne Win.
1964–1967	Aung San Suu Kyi attends Oxford University in Great Britain.
1972	Aung San Suu Kyi marries Michael Aris.
April 1988	Aung San Suu Kyi returns to Myanmar to care for her mother.
August 8, 1988	Mass protests against the government of Myanmar take place.
August 26, 1988	Aung San Suu Kyi gives her first public speech supporting the democracy movement in Myanmar.
July 1989–July 1995	Aung San Suu Kyi is placed under house arrest by the Burmese government.

October 14, 1991	Aung San Suu Kyi is awarded the Nobel Peace Prize.
March 27, 1999	Michael Aris dies.
September 2003– November 2010	Aung San Suu Kyi is placed under house arrest again.
2012	Aung San Suu Kyi is elected to a seat in the Burmese parliament.
2016	Aung San Suu Kyi is appointed state counselor and foreign minister by the Burmese parliament.
2017	Following elections, Aung San Suu Kyi's party retains a majority of seats in the Burmese parliament.

bogyoke The word for "general" in Burmese.

civil disobedience The act of deliberately disobeying a law one thinks to be unjust.

colonial power A country that gains complete control over another for the purpose of using its natural resources.

coup The sudden and illegal seizure of power from an established government by a rival group of individuals.

daw The word for "aunt" in Burmese, often used as a title of affection or respect.

dissident One who publicly dissents from official government policy.

dynasty A form of government in which power passes from parents to their children.

ethnic cleansing A government campaign to force an entire ethnic group from a nation.

fascism An authoritarian government based on nationalism in which power is usually held by a single party or dictator.

human rights The idea that all human beings have certain rights that cannot be taken away from them.

junta A military group that seizes power and rules a nation by force.

martial law Rule by the military.

monsoon A seasonal wind in Asia that brings rain or dry weather.

nationalism A strong dedication to one's own country. Sometimes this may also be the belief that one's own country is superior to others.

nonviolence The idea that people should use peaceful means to achieve political change.

pagoda A Buddhist temple in the shape of a tiered tower.

prisoner of conscience Someone who is imprisoned for their beliefs.

sanctions Restrictions placed on a nation's ability to trade with other nations or join international alliances.

socialism A political system in which resources are owned by a larger community or state.

FURTHER INFORMATION

Books

Amnesty International. *Freedom: Stories Celebrating the Universal Declaration of Human Rights.* New York: Broadway Paperbacks, 2011.

Aung San Suu Kyi. *Freedom from Fear and Other Writings.* New York: Penguin Group, 1991.

——. *Letters from Burma.* New York: Penguin Group, 2010.

——. *The Voice of Hope: Conversations with Alan Clements.* New York: Seven Stories Press. 1997.

Videos

"Address of Aung San Suu Kyi to the Asia Society, New York, 2016"

https://www.youtube.com/watch?v=m5Wbda6Z_jc

Watch Aung San Suu Kyi herself discuss the state of Myanmar and answer questions about democratizing her nation.

"Talk to Al Jazeera–Aung San Suu Kyi: 'There Is No Rule of Law'"

https://www.youtube.com/watch?v=eXj9AF_x_s8

Al Jazeera news contextualizes the Rohingya crisis and interviews Aung San Suu Kyi about human rights.

Websites

Aung San Suu Kyi: Facts. Nobel Prize Committee

https://www.nobelprize.org/nobel_prizes/peace/laureates/1991/kyi-facts.html

The Nobel Prize Committee provides a brief summary of Aung San Suu Kyi's life, with links to other material including the acceptance speech given on her behalf by her son, Alexander Aris; photographs; an interview; and the text of her Nobel Lecture.

Burma Center

https://www.burma-center.org

The Burma Center is an international organization promoting education, health care, and economic development in Myanmar.

Myanmar: International Center for Transitional Justice

https://www.ictj.org/our-work/regions-and-countries/burmamyanmar

Find up-to-date information on the crisis surrounding the Rohingya people and efforts on the part of the international community to address that crisis.

UN: Universal Declaration of Human Rights

http://www.un.org/en/universal-declaration-human-rights

This page includes a transcript of the Universal Declaration of Human Rights, along with information on the history of the declaration and the ongoing development of human rights law.

BIBLIOGRAPHY

Albert, Eleanor. "The Rohingya Migrant Crisis." Council on Foreign Relations, January 12, 2017. http://www.cfr.org/burmamyanmar/rohingya-migrant-crisis/p36651.

Aung San Suu Kyi. *Freedom from Fear and Other Writings*. New York: Penguin Group, 1991.

BBC News, Asia. "Profile: Aung San Suu Kyi." December 5, 2016. http://www.bbc.com/news/world-asia-pacific-11685977.

Beech, Hannah. "Aung San Suu Kyi: Burma's First Lady of Freedom." *Time*, December 29, 2010. http://content.time.com/time/magazine/article/0,9171,2040197,00.html.

Caryl, Christian. "Press Freedom in Burma Is Under Attack Again." *Washington Post*, February 6, 2017. https://www.washingtonpost.com/news/democracy-post/wp/2017/02/06/press-freedom-in-burma-is-under-attack-again-and-aung-san-suu-kyi-isnt-doing-anything-about-it/?utm_term=.a31a9877b6d1.

Economist. "Aung San Suu Kyi Fails to Calm Myanmar's Ethnic Violence." December 24, 2016. http://www.economist.com/news/asia/21712162-ending-it-will-need-far-more-courage-aung-san-suu-kyi-fails-calm-myanmars-ethnic-violence.

Emont, Jon. "Is This the Real Aung San Suu Kyi?" *New Republic*, December 22, 2016. https://newrepublic.com/article/139476/ real-aung-san-suu-kyi.

Griffiths, James. "Is the Lady Listening? Aung San Suu Kyi Accused of Ignoring Myanmar's Muslims." CNN, November 25, 2016. http://www.cnn.com/2016/11/17/asia/myanmar-rohingya-aung-san-suu-kyi/.

Hammer, Joshua. "Aung San Suu Kyi: Burma's Revolutionary Leader." *Smithsonian Magazine*, September 2012. http://www.smithsonianmag.com/people-places/aung-san-suu-kyi-burmas-revolutionary-leader-17728151/.

Hoge, Warren. "Michael V. Aris, 53, Dies: Scholarly Husband of Laureate." *New York Times*, March 30, 1999. http://www.nytimes.com/1999/03/30/world/michael-v-aris-53-dies-scholarly-husband-of-laureate.html.

Holliday, Ian. *Burma Redux: Global Justice and the Quest for Political Reform in Myanmar.* New York: Columbia University Press, 2011.

Holmes, Oliver. "Nobel Laureates Warn Aung San Suu Kyi Over 'Ethnic Cleansing' of Rohingya." *Guardian*, December 30, 2016. https://www.theguardian.com/world/2016/dec/30/nobel-laureates-aung-san-suu-kyi-ethnic-cleansing-rohingya.

Human Rights Watch. "Burma." Retrieved March 1, 2017. https://www.hrw.org/asia/Burma.

New York Times. "Daw Aung San Suu Kyi." Retrieved March 1, 2017. https://www.nytimes.com/topic/person/daw-aung-san-suu-kyi.

Nobel Prize Committee. "Aung San Suu Kyi: Biographical." Retrieved March 1, 2017. http://www.nobelprize.org/nobel_prizes/peace/laureates/1991/kyi-bio.html.

Pederson, Rena. *The Burma Spring: Aung San Suu Kyi and the New Struggle for the Soul of a Nation.* New York: Pegasus Books, 2015.

Popham, Peter. *The Lady and the Peacock: The Life of Aung San Suu Kyi.* New York: The Experiment, LLC., 2011.

Tucker, Shelby. *Burma: The Curse of Independence.* Sterling, VA: Pluto Press, 2001.

United for Human Rights. "Daw Aung San Suu Kyi." Retrieved March 1, 2017. http://www.humanrights.com/voices-for-human-rights/daw-aung.html.

UN News Centre. "UN Rights Expert Calls on Myanmar Authorities to Protect Rohingya Population." February 27, 2017. http://www.un.org/apps/news/story.asp?NewsID=56245#.WNWwJrRzyhA.

Vrieze, Paul. "Humanitarian Situation Worsens in Myanmar." IRIN News, February 21, 2017. https://www.irinnews.org/analysis/2017/02/21/humanitarian-situation-worsens-myanmar-despite-aung-san-suu-kyi.

Wintle, Justin. *The Perfect Hostage: A Life of Aung San Suu Kyi, Burma's Prisoner of Conscience.* New York: Skyhorse Publishing, 2007.

INDEX

Page numbers in **boldface** are illustrations. Entries in **boldface** are glossary terms.

AFPFL, 37–38

Aris, Michael, 14–16, 52, 54–56, 58–59, 62, 64, 66, 70–71, 75–78, **77**, 81–83, **82**

Aung San
  assassination, 38–39
  childhood, 28–30
  family, 35–38, **37**
  independence and, 16, 30, 32, 37–38
  university years, 30–31
  World War II and, 32–35

Aung San Suu Kyi

Aung San and, 16, 40, 51, 59, 65
  awards and tributes, 20, 76–78, 84, **84**, 94–95
  criticism of, 20–21, **72**, 78–83, **79**, 88
  early life, 13, 36–43, **37**, **40**
  education, 14, 42–44, 50–52, 59–60

government service, 20–21, **89**, 90, 92–93, 96–97, **97**
  house arrest, 20, 41, 67, 70–71, 73–78, 83, 87–88
  interest in literature, 14–15, 42–43, 51, 59–60
  marriage, 14–16, 52, 54–56, 75, 82–83
  1988–1989 activism, 8–13, 17–19, 60–67, **61**
  1990s activism, **72**, 78–83, **79**
  nonviolence and, 9–11, 19, 21, 51, 62, 66, 69, 77, 80
  years abroad, 13–16, 43–44, 46–47, 49–56, 58–60

Bangladesh, 90–91, **91**
Bhutan, 52, 54–56, **55**, 58
bogyoke, 33, 35, 39, 41, 44, 53–54, 59, 64–65
Bono, 94–95, **94**
BSPP, 8, 46
Buddhism, 14, 24–26, 29, 39, 52, 54–55, 74, 85–87, 90–92, 96, 98

Bush, Laura, 20, 84

China, 23, 26–27
Clinton, Hillary, 83–84, 88
colonial power, 25–28
coup, 45–46

Danubyu, 5–6, 9–13, 18, 67
daw, 8, 12
dissident, 6
Dobama Asiayone, 31, 45
dynasty, 25, 27

ethnic cleansing, 92, 96, 98

fascism, 32–33
Freedom from Fear, 81, 98

Gandhi, Mahatma, 27, 32, 51, 68–69, **68**, 75

Htin Kyaw, 96
hunger strike, 70–71

Insein Prison, 70, 83

junta, 6, 46, 76, 78, 85, 8–89, 92

Khin Kyi, 16–17, 35–44, **37**, 46–47, 50–52, 54–56, 59–63, 66–67, 73, 75
King, Martin Luther, 69, 80

martial law, 9–10, 66
monks, 29, 31, 54, 85–88, **86**
monsoon, 5
Myanmar
    British rule, 7, 25–27, **26**, **27**, 31–33, 37–38
    culture, 23–25
    democracy, 89–90, 93, 96–97
    geography, 23, **24**
    independence, 16, 37–39
    junta, 45–47, 51, 53–54, 56–59, 70–71, 75–83
    1988–1989 uprising, 8–13, 17–18, 60–67, **61**, **67**, 70–71
    Rohingya crisis, 90–93, **91**, 96–97
    Saffron Revolution, 85–88, **87**

terminology, 7
World War II, 32–37

nationalism, 27, 30, 32, 45, 69
Ne Win, 6–8, 45–47, **45**, 51, 54, 58, 63–64, 66–67, 71
NLD, 6, 8–12, 66, 76, 81, 90, 97–98
Nobel Peace Prize, 20, 76–78, **77**, 93
nonviolence, 9–11, 19, 21, 27, 32, 51, 62, 66, 68–69, 77, 80
Nu, U, 39, 41, 46

Obama, Barack, **89**, 96
Oxford University, 14, **14**, 50–51, 58

pagoda, **22**, 25, 39, 64
prisoner of conscience, 83

Rohingya, 90–93, **91**, 96, 98

sanctions, 85, 88
Saw, U, 39
Saw Maung, 76, 78

Shwedagon Pagoda, **22**, 39, **61**, 64
SLORC, 7, 66, 76
socialism, 30, 46
Soe Tin, U, 53
Sun Yat-sen, 27

Thant, U, 52–53, **53**
Thein Sein, 89

United Nations, 14, 52–54, 60, **97**, 98
U2, 94–95

"Walk On," 94–95
White Bridge Massacre, 61–62

Yangon, University of, 26–27, **27**, 30–31, 45, 60–61

ABOUT THE AUTHOR

Patrice Sherman is the author of several books for young readers, on topics ranging from colonial America to the history of electricity. Her picture book *Ben and the Emancipation Proclamation* won the 2011 Once Upon a World Award from the Simon Wiesenthal Center in Los Angles. She has been a member of Amnesty International for many years. She currently lives in Cambridge, Massachusetts, where she works as a freelance writer. You can find out more about her at her website: www.patricesherman.com.